# NUCLEAR POWER

© Aladdin Books Ltd

*Designed and produced by*
Aladdin Books Ltd
70 Old Compton St
London W1

*First published in the
United States 1985 by*
Gloucester Press
387 Park Avenue South
New York, 10016

ISBN 0531 034887

*Printed in Belgium*

Photographic credits:
Cover and page 27, Science Photo Library;
page 8, Colorific; page 10, Zefa; pages 13, 17,
18, 22 and 25, United Kingdom Atomic Energy
Authority; pages 14, 21 and 29 Frank
Spooner.

The cover picture shows implosion and
energy release in a laser fusion experiment.

J
621.48
MCK
1. Nuclear power
C

## ENERGY TODAY

# NUCLEAR POWER

## ROBIN McKIE

Illustrated by
**Ron Hayward Associates
and Mike Saunders**

Consultant
**Stuart Boyle**

**Gloucester Press**
New York : Toronto

# Introduction

It is easy to forget how important energy is to us all. We need it for heating and lighting our houses, schools and offices and for fueling our cars, trains and aircraft. Industries need energy to make their products. This book looks at ways of getting energy from nuclear power.

Nuclear power is our most powerful energy resource. It can be used to generate electricity and drive huge ships. But it has many opponents who believe that it will always remain a danger to the world.

Sunset over electricity cables in Montreal, Canada

# Contents

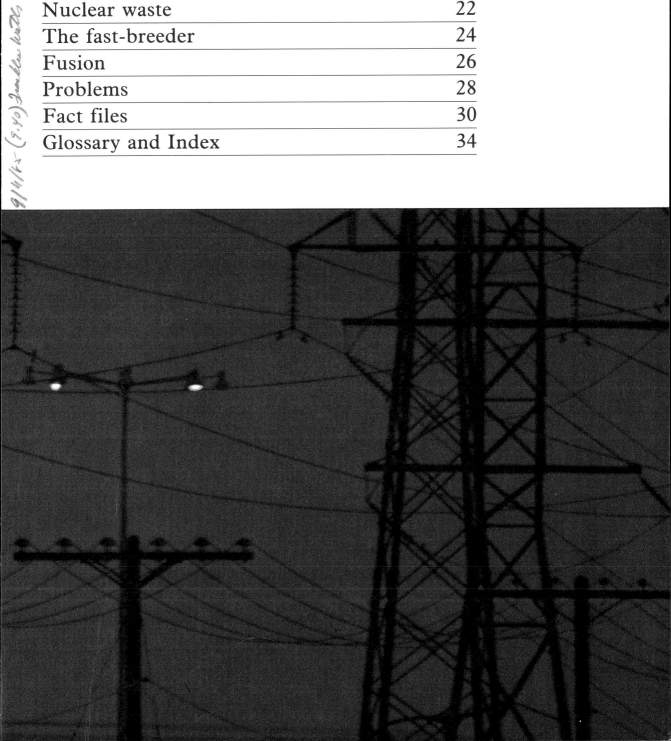

# Nuclear power

Nuclear energy has changed our world. It has been used to make very powerful bombs. But it has also given us a new way of making electricity for our homes and factories.

Coal, oil and gas will run out one day. That is why many countries want to build nuclear power stations. And although these power stations are expensive to build, they are quite cheap to run. Nuclear power was discovered only 40 years ago. Now more than 20 countries use it.

A West German nuclear power station

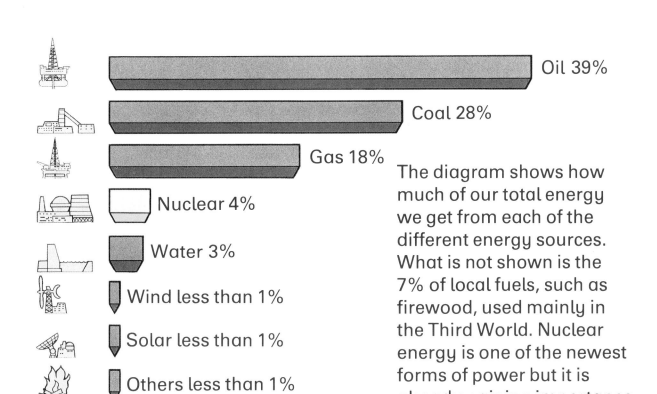

Oil 39%

Coal 28%

Gas 18%

Nuclear 4%

Water 3%

Wind less than 1%

Solar less than 1%

Others less than 1%

The diagram shows how much of our total energy we get from each of the different energy sources. What is not shown is the 7% of local fuels, such as firewood, used mainly in the Third World. Nuclear energy is one of the newest forms of power but it is already gaining importance.

# Splitting the atom

Every object in the world is made up of tiny particles called "atoms." In 1939 scientists discovered how to split the atom.

They found that atoms of a metal called uranium would split into two. This splitting is called "fission." It produces great heat. During fission the atoms throw out even smaller particles called "neutrons."

These neutrons crash into other atoms and break them apart. This whole process is called a "chain reaction," and produces the constant heat needed to make electricity. This happens in the "reactor" room (shown opposite), of a nuclear power station.

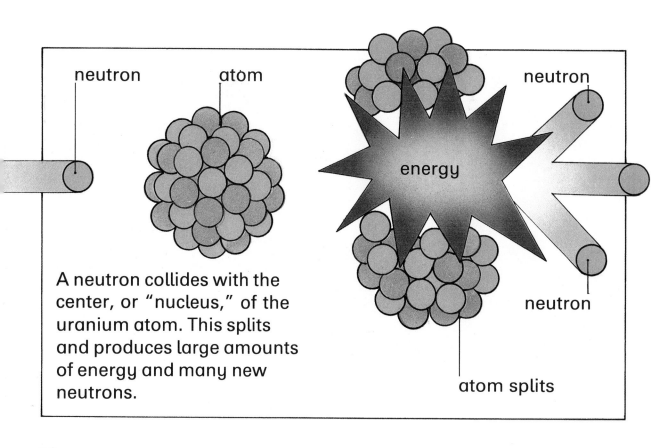

neutron    atom    neutron

energy

neutron

A neutron collides with the center, or "nucleus," of the uranium atom. This splits and produces large amounts of energy and many new neutrons.

atom splits

# Inside the reactor

At the center of a nuclear reactor is the core. This looks like a big drum, and contains "fuel rods." These are full of uranium, the fuel most often used to make nuclear power.

Around these flow a "coolant." This can be gas or water. This coolant carries the heat given off by the rods to a heat-exchanger. Here it is used to boil water into steam. The steam is then blasted against huge turbine blades like the one in the picture. As these turn, they drive "generators," which generate, or make, electricity.

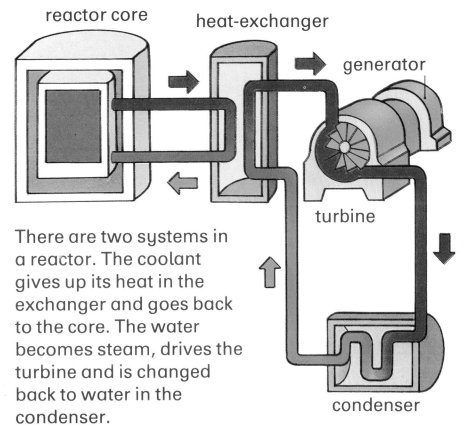

reactor core
heat-exchanger
generator
turbine
condenser

There are two systems in a reactor. The coolant gives up its heat in the exchanger and goes back to the core. The water becomes steam, drives the turbine and is changed back to water in the condenser.

# The reactor core

The coolant carries heat away from the core. But the heat from the reaction still needs to be controlled. Surrounding the fuel rods with water or graphite helps. This is the "moderator." There is also a second set of rods. These are the "control" rods. When they are lowered into the core, they slow the reaction down. The photograph shows control rods being placed inside a core which is being built.

The core of the nuclear reactor is also surrounded by thick walls of concrete and steel. These walls form a shield against deadly rays. These are given off by the reaction in the fuel rods, and we call these harmful rays "radiation."

Inside a nuclear reactor core

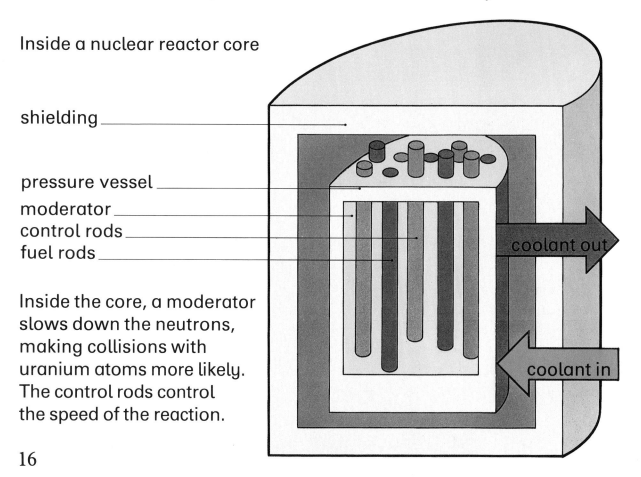

shielding

pressure vessel

moderator

control rods

fuel rods

coolant out

coolant in

Inside the core, a moderator slows down the neutrons, making collisions with uranium atoms more likely. The control rods control the speed of the reaction.

# Working with radiation

So a working nuclear reactor produces both heat and radiation. Radiation cannot be seen or touched. But it is dangerous. Material which gives off radiation is called "radioactive." People exposed to radioactive material can become very ill. It can cause serious diseases such as cancer.

Operating the robot hands

The people who work in a nuclear reactor must be protected. They wear special clothes and are often checked to make sure they are well. They do not touch the radioactive fuel rods. They work behind walls with thick glass windows, and they control long "robot" arms which handle the radioactive fuel rods.

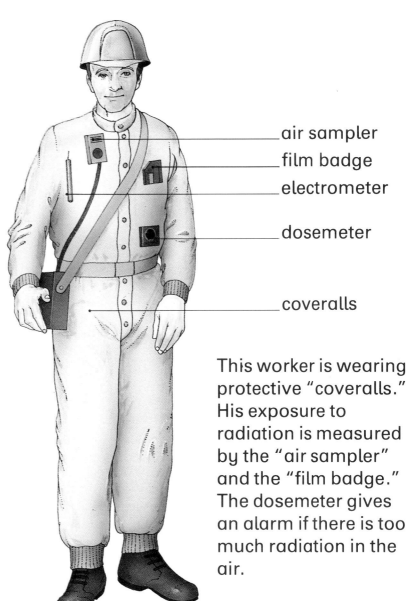

air sampler
film badge
electrometer

dosemeter

coveralls

This worker is wearing protective "coveralls." His exposure to radiation is measured by the "air sampler" and the "film badge." The dosemeter gives an alarm if there is too much radiation in the air.

# Reprocessing

The uranium in the nuclear reactor gets used up very slowly. As it is used up, "spent" fuel rods are left behind. Reacting uranium produces a new substance called plutonium, and also waste material.

Uranium and plutonium can be recovered from the spent fuel rods and used again. This job is carried out in a "reprocessing" plant. The people who work there sometimes practice wearing special emergency clothing, as you can see in the photograph. This is because after reprocessing, a small amount of very dangerous, "high-level" waste material is left behind.

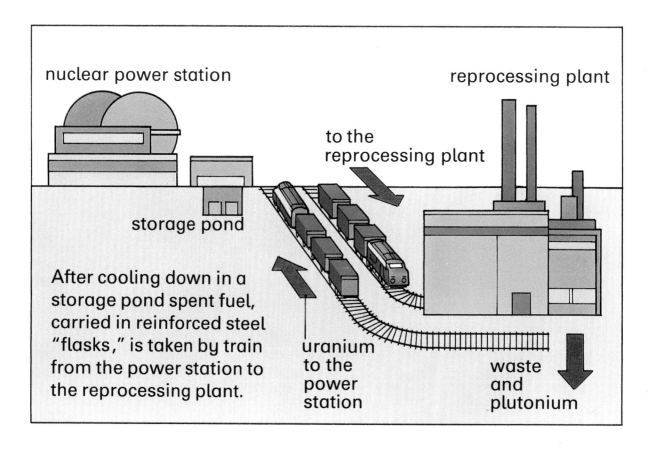

nuclear power station

reprocessing plant

to the reprocessing plant

storage pond

After cooling down in a storage pond spent fuel, carried in reinforced steel "flasks," is taken by train from the power station to the reprocessing plant.

uranium to the power station

waste and plutonium

Nuclear workers wearing special emergency clothing

# Nuclear waste

Nuclear waste is so dangerous that it cannot just be thrown away. Some waste is dumped at sea or buried beneath the earth. High-level waste is the most dangerous of all because it stays radioactive for many years. It is usually stored above ground in thick steel tanks. Some scientists are trying to mix this waste with sand, which would then be melted into a sort of glass. This would still have to be buried deep under the ground.

Drums of waste waiting to be dumped at sea

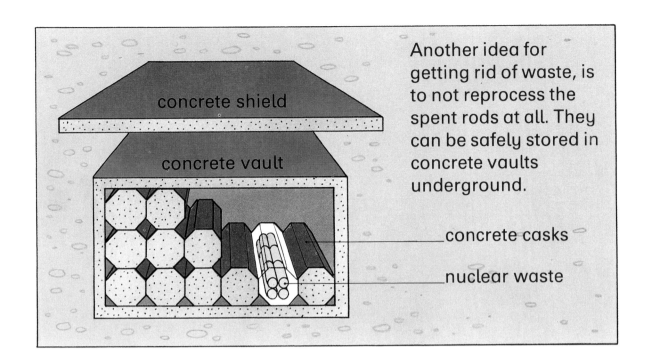

concrete shield

concrete vault

Another idea for getting rid of waste, is to not reprocess the spent rods at all. They can be safely stored in concrete vaults underground.

concrete casks

nuclear waste

# The fast-breeder

Most nuclear reactors make electricity by using uranium. But uranium, before it can be made into reactor fuel, has to be dug out of the ground. One day, the world's supply of uranium will run out.

However, there is another type of reactor. This makes electricity by using plutonium. It has no moderator to slow the neutrons down, and it makes more fuel than it can use. It is called a "fast-breeder."

Fast-breeders are expensive to build. Scientists are still trying to improve them. The one shown in the photograph is at Dounreay, in Scotland.

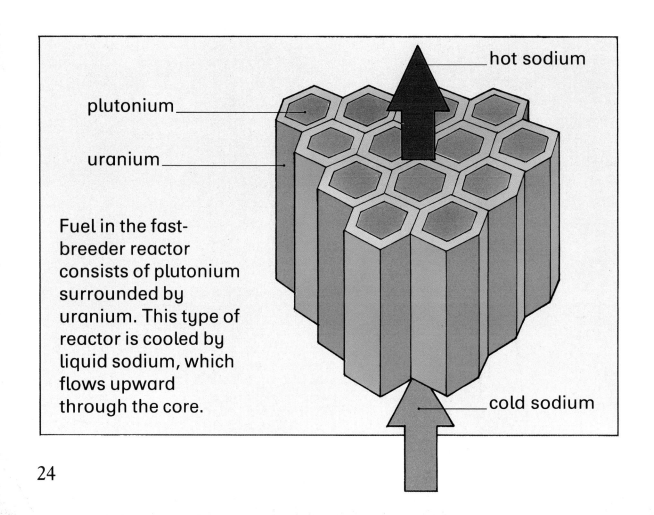

plutonium

uranium

hot sodium

cold sodium

Fuel in the fast-breeder reactor consists of plutonium surrounded by uranium. This type of reactor is cooled by liquid sodium, which flows upward through the core.

# Fusion

We know that atoms produce heat when they break up. But they also produce energy when they join up with other atoms. This is called "fusion." It is fusion that has kept the sun burning for billions of years. However, before atoms will fuse together, they must be heated to almost one hundred million degrees Celsius!

Experiments with "lasers" are being carried out to try to reach such high temperatures. The photograph shows a structure scientists have built to try out one of these experiments. This experiment is called Tosca.

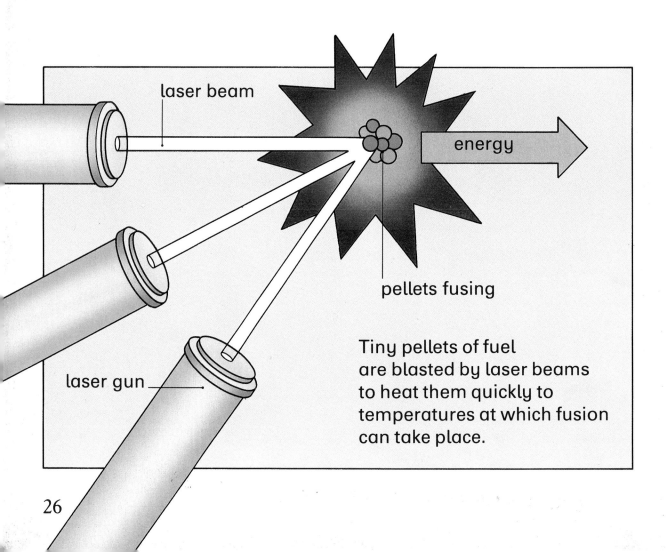

laser beam

energy

pellets fusing

laser gun

Tiny pellets of fuel are blasted by laser beams to heat them quickly to temperatures at which fusion can take place.

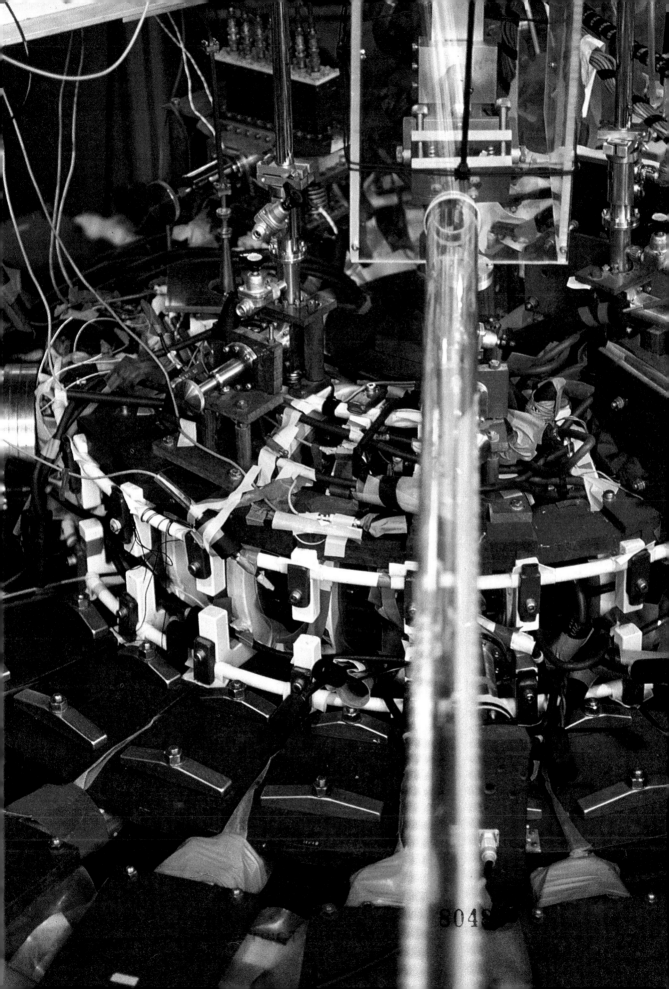

# Problems

The engineers who build nuclear power plants try to make them as safe as possible. But some accidents have happened, and there have been leaks of radiation.

There is also the danger of a "meltdown." This could happen if a reactor lost its supply of cooling gas or water. The core would overheat, melt and break out of its walls.

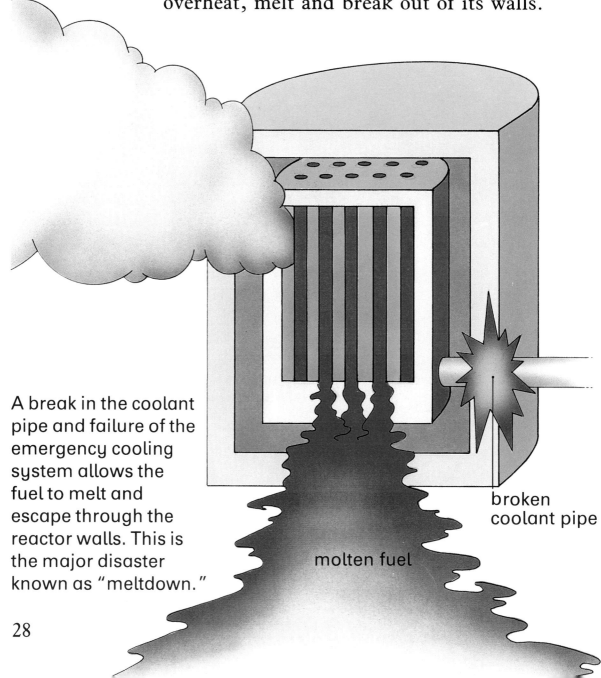

A break in the coolant pipe and failure of the emergency cooling system allows the fuel to melt and escape through the reactor walls. This is the major disaster known as "meltdown."

molten fuel

broken coolant pipe

Some people think nuclear power is both too dangerous and too expensive. There are often demonstrations against it.

But there are good reasons for using nuclear electricity. It can be produced fairly cleanly, and is an extra source of power. Some countries, like France and Belgium, would like to make nuclear energy their main source of power.

Anti-nuclear demonstrators

# Fact file 1

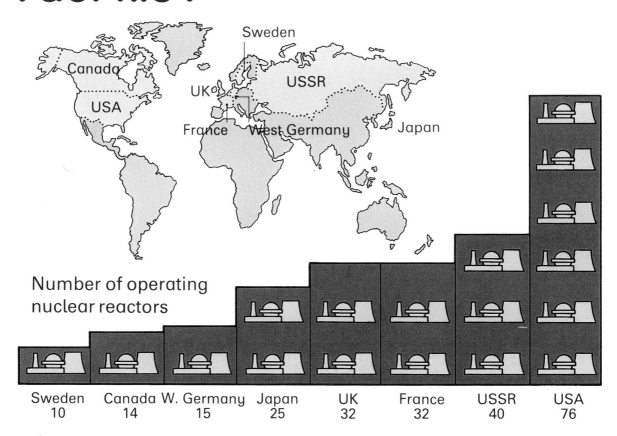

Number of operating nuclear reactors

| Sweden | Canada | W. Germany | Japan | UK | France | USSR | USA |
|--------|--------|-----------|-------|-----|--------|------|-----|
| 10 | 14 | 15 | 25 | 32 | 32 | 40 | 76 |

The world now has 270 nuclear reactors. The map and the diagram above show the major users of nuclear power.

France, Belgium and Finland get almost half their electricity from nuclear power. The USA, with Canada, the UK and West Germany all get about a sixth each from this source.

Nuclear energy may not suit some developing countries, especially if they lack a large electricity grid to distribute it around the country.

Europe (below) contains all those countries that rely on nuclear power for more than 20% of their energy needs.

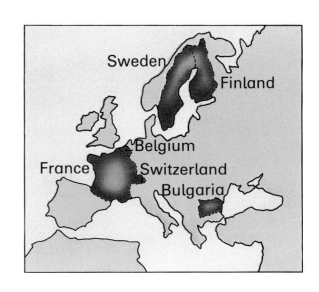

There are two main types of nuclear reactor. The big difference is in the coolant used. Water-cooled reactors (PWRs) are the most popular. Gas-cooled reactors (AGRs), used in the UK and Canada are more expensive to run.

In the core of a PWR (right), water provides both the coolant and the moderator.

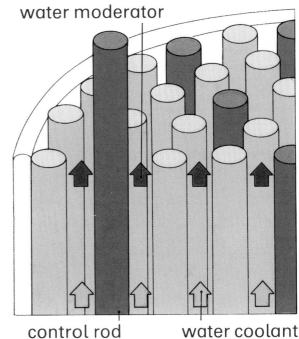

water moderator

control rod          water coolant

Uranium found naturally is not all the same. It is a mixture of different kinds of uranium called isotopes. But only one, U-235, can be used for the fission reaction. The rest of uranium is nearly all U-238, which is also in the fuel rods.

Uranium is an incredibly concentrated source of power. One gramme (one third of an ounce), burned in a reactor, contains as much energy as 3 tonnes (3.30 tons) of coal. One fuel pin is equal to 150 tonnes (165 tons) of coal.

Fuel rods, that are packed into the core of the nuclear reactor, are made up of long pellets of uranium called "fuel pins."

It has been calculated that the energy demands of an average person during a lifetime may equal 350 tonnes (385 tons) of coal. This is equivalent to just 2½ fuel pins – and there can be 200 pins in a single fuel rod.

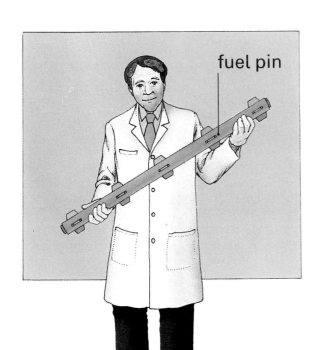

fuel pin

# Fact file 2

Nuclear reactors can be used to produce radioactive isotopes. These are used in medicine, industry and scientific research.

Radioactive isotopes "decay" to give off a penetrating form of radiation. This is used in the treatment of cancer. The rays are used to kill cancerous cells.

Alpha, Beta and Gamma are the names of different forms of radiation. Gamma rays are the most dangerous, and can pass through very thick concrete. Alpha particles do not penetrate far, while Beta particles can just penetrate our skin. But both are deadly if they should get in the mouth.

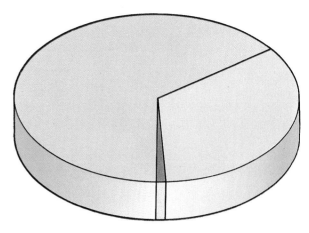

Types of radiation

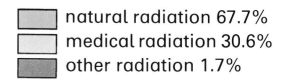

◻ natural radiation 67.7%
◻ medical radiation 30.6%
◻ other radiation 1.7%

Radiation exists in many forms. A lot of it is produced quite naturally from the rays of the sun. It is only exposure to too much radiation that harms us.

Medical X rays are our second source of exposure. But this of course, is strictly controlled, and happens only in hospitals and clinics.

Where does the other 1.7% come from? Some remains from testing bombs, and a tiny amount does escape from reactors.

Working with radiation, though, is very dangerous. The effects of radiation depend on its strength, and the length of exposure.

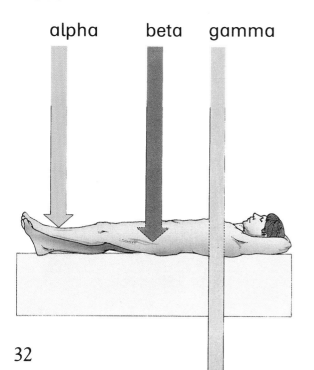

alpha    beta    gamma

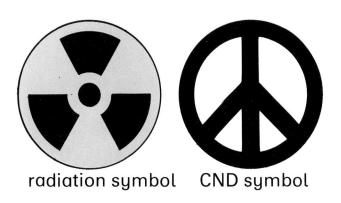

radiation symbol    CND symbol

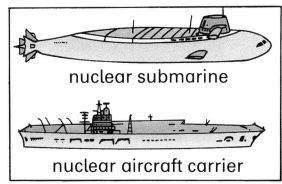

nuclear submarine

nuclear aircraft carrier

Emblems of an argument: the symbols of nuclear radiation (left) and the Campaign for Nuclear Disarmament (right). These highlight the great debate in the world on the subject of nuclear power.

Military uses add to the argument. Nuclear submarines and aircraft carriers can travel great distances on very little power. Nuclear weapons of different kinds are being developed all the time.

Waste is created by both nuclear and coal-fired power stations. But the diagram below shows the different amounts produced. Much nuclear waste can be reprocessed. But this job is extremely dangerous.

Mining for uranium creates more problems. The landscape is not only scarred by the mine but the uranium – safe in its natural condition while below the earth – is dangerous once out of the ground.

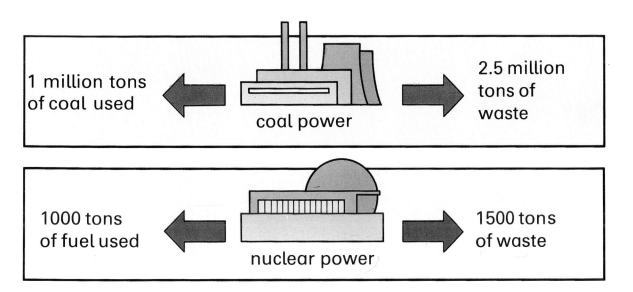

1 million tons of coal used    ←    coal power    →    2.5 million tons of waste

1000 tons of fuel used    ←    nuclear power    →    1500 tons of waste

# Glossary

**Control rods** Inside a nuclear reactor, rods are used to slow down or speed up the reaction taking place.

**Coolant** Gas or liquid that takes heat away from a reactor.

**Core** The heart of a reactor where fuel is turned into energy.

**Enrichment** Process of increasing the proportion of isotopes that will cause fission.

**Fast-breeder** A reactor that makes more plutonium fuel than it uses.

**Fission** The splitting of an atom into fragments. This releases energy.

**Isotopes** Different forms of the same element.

**Plutonium** A substance made inside a reactor. Plutonium can also be used as a nuclear fuel.

**Radiation** Rays and particles given off by substances inside a nuclear reactor.

**Reprocessing** Process for removing uranium and plutonium from waste fuel.

# Index

**Acknowledgements**
*The publishers wish to thank the following organisations who have helped in the preparation of this book:*
Central Electricity Generating Board UK, Culham Laboratories (Abingdon, Oxfordshire), Electricity Council (Overseas Division), Friends of the Earth, Ministry of Defence, Science Research Council – The Rutherford and Appleton Energy Laboratory UK, UK Department of Energy.

PRINTED IN BELGIUM BY

INTERNATIONAL BOOK PRODUCTION